FALLING
FROM
SILENCE

FALLING
FROM
SILENCE

POEMS

David R. Slavitt

Louisiana State University Press

Baton Rouge   2001

Copyright © 1999, 2000, 2001 by David Slavitt
All rights reserved
Manufactured in the United States of America
First printing
10 09 08 07 06 05 04 03 02 01
5 4 3 2 1

Designer: Barbara Neely Bourgoyne
Typeface: Sabon
Printer and binder: Thomson-Shore, Inc.

Library of Congress Cataloging-in-Publication Data
Slavitt, David R., 1935–
    Falling from silence : poems / David R. Slavitt.
        p. cm.
    ISBN 0-8071-2672-1 (cloth : alk. paper) — ISBN 0-8071-2673-X (paper : alk. paper)
    I. Title

PS3569.L3 F35 2001
811'.54—dc21

                                                                                00-048555

The author offers grateful acknowledgment to the editors of the following journals, in
which some of these poems first appeared, sometimes in slightly different form: *Cort-
land Review* (an internet journal), *Hudson Review, Midstream, New Criterion, Pivot,
Poetry, Shenandoah,* and *Texas Review.*
    "The Battle against Humbaba," "At Snowbird," and "Cape Cod Beach" appeared
in *Bright Pages: Yale Writers 1701–2001* (Yale, 2001). "Jackson Pollack's *Number 13A:
Arabesque*" appeared in *A Gallery of Poets* (Yale University Art Gallery, 2001)

The paper in this book meets the guidelines for permanence and durability of the
Committee on Production Guidelines for Book Longevity of the Council on Library
Resources. ∞

for Gina and Bernard Gotfryd

CONTENTS

I

Glimpse

If the stain of an instant's sin endures forever,
may a moment of grace not also transcend time
to make its mark in eternity's ledger? Beauty—

of an egret's stately posture, a blossoming tree's
dance, or a moonlight-silvered sea's repose—
is an instant's transaction we try to remember. And fail.

But we can be objects of connoisseurs' scrutiny, too,
reaching heights we never noticed ourselves,
who were, or will be, for that redeeming instant,

handsome, gorgeous, or heartbreakingly cute,
even the homeliest of us. At three? At ninety?
In repose in lamplight, reading? Or, later, bone-tired,

asleep in the chair? But the hardest and saddest cases . . .
What the inattentive observer, the unskilled eye,
the insufficiently generous soul may miss

is the glimpse in the black of night, or in dreams (his, hers,
or God's), of how it ought to have been: there is beauty
to make the angels, singing its praises, gasp.

The Valve

The one-way flow of time we take for granted,
but what if the valve is defective? What if the threads
on the stem wear thin, or the stuffing box or the bonnet
ring leaks, or the joints to the pipe ring fail,
and there's a backwash?
                              It happens.

                                        And then old loves,
meeting again, have no idea what to do,
resuming or not resuming from where they were
years before. Or the dead come back to chat.
Or you are reduced for a giddy moment to childhood's
innocent incompetence. You look up
as if to see some hint in the sky's blackboard.
But then, whatever it was, some fluff or grit
that clogged the works, works free, and again time passes,
almost as before, and you try to get on with your life.

Prophecy

Think of a sneeze you know is coming, that tickle,
that disagreeable leaching away of control
over what you were doing, but larger, and worse. Think of

that vagal sensation you have in the dark, hung over,
kneeling on bathroom tiles when you know your stomach
will one of these moments erupt and send it all back.

That's what it felt like for Mopsus, Calchas, the rest. . . .
Or sex, just before you come, when the ground you lie on
is giving way, is opening up like a grave.

Worms

That pair of cradle vipers Hercules
strangled returns intent on vengeance to bite
adults defenseless against the mortal squeeze
of their relentless coils of appetite:

the prick or cunt, and the gut. And there is no
escape, as Eve discovered or knew from the start.
Resist as we may, those worms will work their woe
on the noblest soul, corrupting the purest heart

and destroying flesh itself in a nihilist's pride.
The warnings of doctors and common sense you ignore
to gorge, as if you hungered for suicide,

or, at the other's perseverant prompting, in more
sordid encounters that leave you unsatisfied,
you abase yourself to panderer or whore.

Airedales

Those who did it are dead now. And what they did,
they were trained to do and had no choice, no freedom.
Still, when I read in some book review that the camps'
guard dogs were "Alsatians, Airedales, and Doberman
pinschers," I can't help blaming the dogs of these breeds,
even though they have no idea what breeds they are.

Alsatians? Of course. And Dobermans? They are weapons
that sometimes wag their tails. But Airedales?
                                                    Yappy
clowns they are, huge terriers after all.
Frisky perhaps . . . But then the zebra-suited
Musselmänner didn't think they were cute
as they watched the attacks of those packs of killer dogs.

But the National Association for the Advancement
of Airedales? And the Airedale Anti-Defamation League?
And the liberal line that says I cannot blame
a class for what some members may have done?
They are all correct, as I admit at once.
But I would cross the street to avoid an Airedale.
And I would not have an Airedale in my house.

Fruit Cart

Not words anymore, but a call a bird might make
for a mate or to stake its claim to territory,
at his fruit stand in the Ninth Street market, he croaks,
"Emeneep," and then, as the neurons fire again,
"emeneep."
                    The years have worn his vocal cords
coarse as the iteration has worn his words
to syllables all but cleansed of sense: "How many?"

A loss? Or may one call it a giving away,
a sloughing off of inessentials? The message
is clearer, blurred, a calling out for attention:
Here! Listen! Look! Emeneep! Buy!

The Weight of the Spirit

With much glass tubing and flashing arcs, the not-
quite loony doctor in his white coat essays
the problem of spirit and matter: he has got
enormous delicate scales on which he weighs

the dying and dead, hoping thus to find
by how many grams or grains it is that the spirit,
departing, diminishes corpses. Or ask whether mind
weighs a bit more than the dead brain does (I fear it

may be a different but similar question)? Still,
I brood about these things, often late at night.
As I'm drifting off, there's an inner self that will
settle, palpably falling away to the right

and behind me—no matter how I am lying in bed.
A smaller, simpler creature, rather better
than I am, it is not quite happily wed
to me, or is stuck with me, or to me. Let our

selves be startled, as when we say we've had
a turn, and I can feel it try to adjust.
I am the baggy suit through which the sad
clown must display his grace in that sawdust

where elephants just performed. Sometimes in panic,
it loosens its grip, or, very rarely, in bliss.
When I am not quite myself, depressed or manic,
I feel its letting go. What remains of me is

negligible, and knows it, is bereft
and at the same time indifferent. It obeys
instructions the departed spirit left
before it left. Exactly what it weighs,

those scientists never determined. As soon ask why
when a magnet is demagnetized, the metal's

loss is only of meaning. When I die,
I'll know the feeling, as my spirit settles

into its final rest for that long night—
behind me and a little to the right.

Exception

But, in the land of the blind,
where the one-eyed man is king,
when he wears the emperor's new clothes,
he can get away with it.

Privately Owned

for John Fitz Gibbon

At night, on the walls of a house, its paintings dream,
or, say, play in the dreams of those who dwell
among them: on the walls of their minds they hang
or swim in the dark, but then, as a new day dawns,
coming up for air, they surface again to light
and settle into the frames where we think them fixed.

Domestic wildlife, they frisk, while those in museums,
caged, like Schopenhauer's ape or Rilke's
panther, stare down at blank and stupid guards
in whose stolen naps there is no room for greatness
to move in, never mind romp as they also do
in churches, where in parishioners' prayers, those directed

dreams, the shimmering marches of consciousness
offer that unconstrained attention they thrive in.
A glimpse is never enough, as the steady gaze
of scholars, too eager and earnest, is too much.
From a canvas, stretched over time, each stroke of the brush
must make its mark in the slowly roused neuron.

Each daybreak, and every passage along that wall,
indicts, corrects your memory, trains your eye
with tints, textures, and shapes that are not even better
but different, surely, from what you believed with surprises,
ever smaller but nonetheless precious for that,
like a many-years-married couple's allusive banter.

Jackson Pollack's Number 13A: Arabesque

A big mother, which is to say expensive,
it demands a big wallet, a big wall.
For a doodle, a slopping and dripping, on awning cloth,
an imposition of will even more than of talent?
My kid could do that, or my chimpanzee, if I had one!
Well, let them think so and still shell out, big time.

The American art form is self-promotion.
Fame is the game. And Jackson's was solid: Jack
the Dripper. Not even Warhol's soup cans or Johns's
flags could match in shock value Pollack's defiance
of pretty pictures. You hang on a wall something useless
and expensive to show you believe in your taste—these squiggles
in housepainter's enamel, the tracks of a drunken
figure skater, an attempt at randomness
that fails as intelligence reasserts itself.
(His or our own?) Those glints are artifacts
of the glossy paint catching at random the light
of the installation. Up close, they go away.
And "Arabesque"? (Why not? The *Lavender Mist*
has no lavender in it, or mistiness either.)
Spatters, drips, outpourings. An inspired drunk,
a galoot, he was, with a dash, just, of refinement,
a guy smug sons of bitches could patronize
but pay just the same, through the nose, through every pore,
bleeding money.
                                    But what America gives
she charges for. The convertible crashes, and there,
at the end of the road, in glistening viscous red,
are his eloquent signature splatters—his action painting,
the stupid but shrewd intuitive gesture by which
he would keep his art's market healthy for years.

Remarks of Goya's Marquesa de Santa Cruz

What the Marquesa de Santa Cruz is trying to say,
if only they'd shut up for a moment, stand still,
and turn to the right to pay an instant's attention—
but no more than one in a hundred will do that, ignoring
the guides and the eyes of the others, fixed as they are
on the Naked Maja's tits (never mind the spiel,
that talk of the pillows or the white sheet on the greenish
blue of the ottoman: tits are what they stare at)—
is this: that fame, such naked fame, is ugly,
and that she, the Marquesa, prefers things the way they are.
The lyre she holds in her left hand is art, which means
she needs that handkerchief her right hand is clutching
to mop the brow her poet's wreath oppresses,
because beauty will get you only so far; even tits
will get you only so far (her own are fine
and mostly revealed); but somehow, a name, an image,
a gesture takes off to fly on its own, transformed
as those paintings from Godoy's collection, the *Duchess
of Alba,* or maybe not (the heads don't match
the bodies, and both the faces were painted later),
have taken off, soaring up from the Prado wall
to hang in a cartoon sky, ideas of themselves,
as crude as the postcard versions the gift shop sells.
But she is a Goya, too, and her doleful expression—
resignation? distress? disgust?—speaks, if not volumes,
then the thousand words some pictures are worth, if only
those cattle they herd through the room would turn their thick
heads for five seconds for Christ's sake to listen and look.

Ink

Poised above the paper, the pen's nib
is gravid with ink, a tremulous black droplet
by which one can learn to calibrate fluctuations
of weather, inner and outer, as if it were crimson
liquid that lives in thermometers' wells: a poet's
day is not merely his own, for clouds as they drift
across his skies will darken or brighten your own.
Or is it yet stranger? When San Gennaro's dried

blood liquefies in the phial, the people of Naples
offer up prayers of thanks, but the miracle's true
work is within their own hearts, where freshets of faith,
of hope, and even of charity run renewed.
His drop of ink can do that too: it dries
but later flows elsewhere in your tears, your blood.

Pen

In the heft of the pen's shaft in a hand's crotch,
one can feel, as pregnant women must, the weight
of words that shift on the fleshy fulcrum's balance
in that webby place near the base of the thumb: the letters
that danced in the light like gnats will suddenly light
on some twig of a notion a held breath can make tremble
in an unpredictable motion—like this pen's—
that no one would think could bear the fruit of truth.

Notes to the Poems

Too frazzled to focus attention, I riffle pages,
hoping for something soothing or prepossessing,
a nugget or trifle, some truffle. Poems? Too much.

They demand too much, or say I am lacking in faith
for such coherent exchanges. But the notes at the back
offer me toys, trouvés, donnés that engaged

a lively mind, diverting or setting to flight
or to work—that simple grain of sand within
the cultured pearl I'm not now inclined to wear.

Some notes can be pompous, preach or preen, but the best
from the best poets are bright with the joy of children
displaying to one another stones they've found

that the play of the surf has polished and offered up.
To read that "herring prefer to come inshore
on the dark of the moon" can settle one's jangled nerves;

to be told that the adult barnacle is "shrimplike
and glued down by the top of its head" can restore
the right order of things: these are truths I'm learning

as if at a desk again in a distant schoolroom.
"When covered with water, the barnacle rhythmically opens
and closes its trapdoors to extend the six pairs

of feathery cirri like a small hand, grasping blindly
for any planctonic or detrital morsels adrift
in the water." Exactly. A small hand. Grasping blindly.

For Ben, on His 65th Birthday

Birthdays, which used to be pleasant, have lately turned
Equivocal, if not quite hostile—yet.
Noisemakers, candles, and silly hats we have learned
Somehow to suffer, and even enjoy as we get

Our presents—not pricey nouns, but verbs in that tense
No text remains in long. We settle for
Simpler, subtler pleasures intelligence
Commends as we come to learn how less can be more.

Old friend, dear friend, how many the years and how few
The hours that we have shared together! From this,
Consider how crude are clocks to record the true
Heartbeats' log of our lives of pain and bliss.

Ideas

The gods, being immortal, lacked
that seriousness heroes could claim
and merely played at love and war.
What could they lust or battle for
beyond the diversion of a game
that might for a brief while distract

from the longueurs of eternity?
Ideas, which also never die,
are likewise frivolous: they live
half lives in the infinitive
and, like those denizens of high
Olympus, irresponsibly

flutter above us, touching now
and then those mortals whom they choose
to trouble with their equivocal gift
that seems at least at first to lift
our spirits up, redeem, excuse
defects, and give us purpose. How

ennobling this is, though brief,
for circumstance and common sense
assert a qualifying claim,
and even the purest thought turns tame:
degraded by experience,
epiphany fades to mere belief,

or so it seems to us, but they
are disappointed, too, who find
distressing their abrupt descent
into a new environment,
not of the elevated mind
but malleable human clay

that cannot hold them long. And we,
more relieved than not, repair

to mundane appetite that gives
the flesh in which the spirit lives
the grist it cannot get from air,
abstraction, and nobility.

Cruising

Cruising for sensations, as if the right
image in the right light might, for a moment,
make sense of it all. . . .
                            But the world is not a brothel,
and the nerves at last (or sooner than that) go numb.

Then what? In a dismal dawning, as if from mist,
shapes come clear and what you find displaces
whatever it was you were looking for.
                            Disgust,
that harridan you wind up with, time after time,
though not the one you'd have chosen, is nonetheless
not uncongenial, familiar, almost a friend.

In the Maze

You study faces for clues: those you've seen before
are coming back from dead ends and are all smiles,
but fixed, too bright, as they try to conceal (from you?
from themselves?) that growing panic they know is their own
fault for taking the dare of the Hampton Court Palace
maze. It's December and cold, and you'll soon need to pee.
Nobody's running, but, walking smartly and grinning,
we try to appear amused still by the joke

as if we didn't regret a stupid decision,
a series of ruinous choices in what we have known
as an unforgiving world. It's part of the tour,
that fear and the shame they felt that still hangs in the air,
Woolsey's and Thomas More's, and Ann Boleyn's.
And Catherine Howard's. And Lady Jane Gray's. And Mary's.

Hell

Hell is very much like heaven except
that the furniture there has somehow been misarranged,
a pipe in a wall is leaking (the plumber again
has failed to show up), and the freezer compressor is shot
so that food is defrosting, and where is that serviceman?

Such trivial things! Surely, the great-souled and wise
seem not to mind, while we, other and lesser
(but honest about our feelings) . . . do we know better?
And must we keep still? Don't we have the right to complain?
But where is a pen that works? And where are my glasses?

The Upas Tree

Wherever it is—if it is, that is—then that
is the middle of nowhere, its lonely habitat,
the ground around it, desolate and bare.
No songbird ventures near its poisoned air;
no bush or fern can grow, or blade of grass—
only itself, the upas tree, which has
such toxic power that nothing else will thrive
within a ten-mile radius or survive
in five, they say, whoever *they* are. Who?
Natives with tales of fools who ventured too
far upriver and, with a tortured breath,
spat warnings of that tree and the terrible death
with which it punishes any who come too close
to the empty place in the jungle where it grows.
A fabrication, perhaps, to keep us out
who have come to exploit and enslave their country? No doubt,
but are we not also intrigued and attracted by
the idea of such a thing and inclined to defy
the natives' superstition? Shall we not go
upcountry, therefore, and paddle for days in the slow,
muddy current, peering at each bend to see
through a gap in the jungle's wall that fabulous tree,
serene in the noxious beauty we can assume
so deadly a thing must have, and a rich perfume
its enormous blossoms pour into empty air
in a vain abundance, for nothing else is there?
In that glade's unholy silence, day and night,
it contemplates itself in a Carmelite
devotion even heaven might envy, sick
of generation and all that spawning of thick
swarms of life so avid for being. This
rejection of the world's abundance is
the exquisite idea that each may reach
after learning all that affirmation can teach.
It is the jungle's dream of the tundra's bare
and gelid abnegation, satiety's prayer
to which we all must say Amen one day.

Upriver, inland, where all the maps give way
to featurelessness, there are many stories told
of abandoned cities or mountains of pure gold,
obvious in their appeal to the vulgar mind,
which is reason to disbelieve them. More refined
and different is that of the upas, which some men
have wondered about and even believed in. When
we approach it, our breathing bated, do we feel
the body's ebbing away? It has an appeal
we never expected but come to appreciate
as we yield ourselves to the single-minded hate
at the root of that tree, its defiance, rejection, and curse
upon everything alive in the universe,
including itself—but, being immune to its own
poison, it has to keep going, albeit alone,
until, one day, there may come from a grudging sky
the lightning bolt it awaits, and it, too, can die.

Arcade Game

The awkwardness is the point, the challenge: control
of the game's mechanical jaws that hover over
its jumble of junky toys is, at best, haphazard,
which gives the objects below in the bin their value
as prizes for luck or skill or some combination.
There is also a time constraint: your coin will buy
no more than so many seconds, as if the machine
were a small formal poem, a quatrain, say,
the meaning of which is always incidental.
You seize whatever you can, as in a poem,
and settle, pleased with your winnings, pleased with yourself.

Cirque

1

The acrobats and jugglers will allow
gravity as possible, one idea
among many but, surely, not the best.

Knowing better, we yearn to believe our eyes:
we feel our spirits rise to play, to pretend
such grace as we could never ourselves have dreamed.

They sport in the air, hang on the music, on strength
and will as far beyond us as above us.
The Saltimbancos' poised defiance of weight

and height and time, to them diverting toys,
basks unashamed in the glare of the crowd's love,
which, by itself, has crushed many lesser men.

From such an exaltation, to have to return
to the common sense of the world is a sorry business.
The stigmata of our applause sting on our palms.

2

As children, gazing up at the glamorous pair
delighting us by cavorting high in the air,
we were right to assume they had to be husband and wife,
sharing the joys and dangers of circus life—
as adults we know how risks outside the tent
are much like those more dramatic and violent
disasters we feared might overtake them above
our heads in their demonstration of married love:

they trusted each other's strength and timing to fly
like angels with spotlights following them and defy
the gravity, time, ennui, and faithlessness
to which the rest of us below confess,
as we recall them, performing night after night
their routines of letting go and holding tight.

Flatbed Wrecker

Salvage any tow truck can manage, but this
is a grander business, salvation, a resurrection,
albeit secular, and therefore we can believe it.
(Is recycling the metempsychosis of objects?)

Their twisted metal, straightened, will shine again.
But first, on the flatbed truck, those willing beasts
we drove so savagely (what else to conclude
from these grotesque and violent conclusions?) now

get to ride, themselves. In the metaphor
they are for once promoted from vehicle to
tenor, the star of the show, the parade's lone float.

If cars could dream, this is what they'd imagine
and yearn for, such a reversal, such elemental
relenting, the effortless motion. And then release.

Cake and Milk

A piece of cake is easy, but taking the cake,
an achievement, commands respect or at least our notice,
like a fine kettle of fish, which may be, as they say,

a horse of a different color. Eating your cake
and having it, too, is a trick worth some attention,
even though one hears that the wrong way round

from half-baked people who honestly think the proof
is in the pudding, *tout court*. (Pudding heads!)
Risen and fallen, we're angels' food and devils',

no matter how you slice it. "Let 'em eat cake,"
Marie Antoinette quipped, saying a mouthful,
or biting off more than she could chew. With icing.

Life's not all cakes and ale, which is hard cheese.
(Do they make that from spilt milk?) You can't go back,
so it's useless to wish your cake were dough again.

Falling from Silence

for Sam

Listening, listening, picking out sounds and phonemes,
patterns of vowels and consonants, objects and actions,
the words that up until now he has not required,
surrounded by babble, in constant cooing and crooning
he floats like a fish in the water or bird in the air,
swooping and soaring at play in an aether of love.

Greetings to a Granddaughter

My welcome, though new to you—as what is not?—
approaches the end of its shelf-life as I do mine:
I hold your seven pounds and eleven ounces,

a breathing chuck roast, roughly. Such malapropos
conceits are better suppressed. If your brother refuses
to utter your name and insists on generic "Baby,"

or your sister wants to cover you up with her blanket
(forever, although she would never say so aloud),
I can as your grandfather address that figment

you mostly will be for years yet, greet you, and beg
pardon for all our deplorable failures of manners
and grace as you rearrange, displace, disturb,

and demand with your tyrannical helplessness
that's hard not to resent. Grudging, we'll manage
to shift, make room for you to grow and, we hope,

prosper. A longer and happier life than my own
I wish you, fretful as I do so, and sorry
for that and all my other shortcomings, and those

of this difficult world into which you have come to adventure.

Bedtime

The vividness of a small child's understanding
fades as you learn to face each dying day
as if that were mere metaphor, as if
it weren't, itself, a piece of your own demise.
The fears that grip the child at bedtime, dread
of the dark and of being alone, you lose for a while,
but they return years later, and now, at sunset,
you feel the darkness pressing upon you. Practice

hasn't helped. The day is ebbing away,
a part of your life, and, lying down in bed,
you try to deny you are doing what invalids do.
In that interval when mind is guttering out,
you listen to sounds of plumbing: water is running,
and there's nothing on earth you can do to turn it off.

Toy

With their simplified shapes and too-bright primary colors,
they do not attempt to persuade but still make bold
to solicit attention (the buyer's? the child's?) and allow
imagination's investment on which the return

could even be love. It's a heavy load for such tiny
trucks to haul, and mostly they fail to deliver,
break down, or lose, for no discernible reason,
their novelty's luster to join on the playroom floor

that clutter of whatever careless, carefree hands
have let fall there. We remember toys we loved;
what's dimmer and hard to recapture is children's indifference.
We had it once, that easy grip that was always

prepared for something better or merely different,
or nothing at all, but that blur in which things will appear
and disappear. As if all tots were Buddhists,
heartless and wise, they know from the first moment

the truck is already broken, and yet are content.

Repetition

Somewhere between the rehearsals and reenactments
there must be—we suppose—a performance we either
perceive or whimsically choose and declare as the real

thing to which past and future, knowing or not,
all along referred. That welter of repetitions
turns out in the end not to have been so free,

as meaning imposes or, like the dumb sun, dawns,
and objects that swam in an indeterminate sea
of diffident potential assume their recalcitrant

shapes. So it is with events we thought we knew
rather too well. Beginnings and endings are clear,
but middles, that murk where significance often lurks,

are tricky, and joy, which ought to be easy enough
to recognize, defies the fastest tripping
shutter or eyelash flutter and, sly, furtive,

shy as a timid child, is abruptly gone,
leaving us searching, rummaging high and low
(those, I'm afraid, are the usual places), looking

for some faint trace or imprint. Exceptional moments?
Diversions, mostly. Experience, where we live,
is lying down each night, disposed the same way

on the same bedding we tidied that morning. The rumples
we smoothed mean more than the wretched or splendid dreams
our souls proposed while our bodies shifted or thrashed.

What's hard to see is whatever the blasé eye
assumes as we tread our daily round: a flash
of red as a cardinal crosses the sky, we'll remark,

looking up, and ignore how our path leads gently downward.

Height

> The question that he frames in all but words
> is what to make of a diminished thing.
> —Robert Frost

My doctor, for some obscure reason, is checking
not only my weight but (he's kidding, right?) my height. . . .
This is for pediatricians, and parents who mark
the growth of their little darlings on door frames. But now
he adjusts the metal rod to the top of my head
and discovers a diminution. I am not, he tells me,
six feet anymore, but five feet ten and a half. . . .
And what (aside from the obvious wise-ass answer)
is the difference?
     I'm not—as I was, as I thought of myself—
tall. I was proud of that height I'd done nothing to earn.
If it simply happened, whatever talent I have
also just happened, as grace does, or love. And now
it's gone. As grace can go, or love. And we do
what we can to accept and adjust. (What choice do we have?)
I'm average. Of middling stature. I stand up as straight
as I can, the way I was taught to do as a boy,
but it doesn't help, won't change me, can't bring back
that not altogether insignificant edge
I used to have. With this slight shift in perspective,
no longer *de haut en bas,* there may be new lessons
I apparently need to learn in humility, faith,
or simply that resignation that age should provide.
A tall order, it may yet come in time.

Woodpile

The firewood stacked alongside the house is wrong,
but where else is there room? Even if there were,
where would I find someone to move it? Arthritic,
too old to do it myself, I temporize. . . .
Maybe the termites will spare us a little longer.
In a month, with a killing frost, we'll have a reprieve
and get through another season. What more can I hope for?
Such shiftlessness (or realistic thinking)
is what I've learned so far, well enough to suspect
that it will get worse as the days nibble away,
hollowing out like termites, like carpenter ants,
what I thought was secure, the structure's beams and timbers.

Two Sonnets of Philippe Desports (1546–1606)

1

Here Icarus, that intrepid fellow, fell.
What daring, to presume to fly on the breath
of the winds! Stripped of his feathers, he dropped to a death
that leaves us saddened, but touched with envy as well

for his happy enterprise. Oh, splendid spirit!
From such a brief disaster, he wrung a great
and apparently endless fame. It's a fortunate fate
that we desire at least as much as we fear it.

On untried paths, his youth was undismayed.
His strength may have failed, but his heart was never afraid.
Eager for that adventure into the sky,

he sought out excellence: his death was brave.
Blue sky, his goal; the blue sea was his grave.
What better aim, or tomb, or way to die?

2

Poor broken heart, having committed no crime
you see how your better part is led away
as if to a dungeon. . . . But stop your groaning, stay
silent and patient throughout this trying time,

and think of the hearts of the world, inconstant all
except to change, to which they could swear to be true.
After a losing spell at the table, a new
spin may give one a better bounce from the ball,

for that's how the world works as Fortune turns
her wheel: after winter's cold, the summer burns;
day follows night; and even the worst storms clear.

Lovers, content till now, find themselves in a state
of distraction, while desperate men, by some quirk of fate,
can be blithe and happy. Relax. And persevere.

The Kiss Repaid

after La Fontaine

M. Guillot, a simple farmer,
took to wife a comely lass.
One day a gentleman happened to pass
who, stricken by this country charmer,
asked, "Would you let me kiss your bride
 if I promised to pay you back one day?"
 Guillot was determined to seem soigné
"She is at your service," he replied.
Seizing the moment and Perronnelle,
the gentleman gave her a sloppy kiss
that the woman accepted, though blushing at this.
A week goes by, and Guillot hears tell
that the man is now married and therefore goes
to collect that kiss the new bridegroom owes
from the bride, who turns out to be gorgeous. With zeal
Guillot embraces the woman, with real
passion . . . and then he stops. *Very well,*
he thinks, *we are quits—though I wish, instead*
of merely kissing my Perronnelle
that day, he had taken her off to bed.

Achilles' Shield

after an anonymous epigram,
Greek Anthology, Book IX, 115

Inanimate objects can seem sometimes to object,
to display animus even, as did that shield
Odysseus won—and Ajax in shame or rage

killed himself. The Greek ships sailed away;
Odysseus' went down with the crew, near Corcyra;
and the shield Hephaistos made for Thetis' son

floated away to wash ashore at last
at Salamis, which was Telamon's island, whose sons
had gone together to Troy—Teucer and Ajax.

Praxilla's Version

Getting the point at last of the boar's tusk,
which is sharper than any of Venus' warnings, Adonis
enters at last that shadowy kingdom where ghosts,
clinging to fading shreds of memory, ask him
what he misses most of all.
                                    And Adonis answers,
"First, the light of the sun, and then the moon
and stars at night. . . ."
                                    "And then?" the sad ghosts prompt.
Adonis thinks. "A plate of sliced cucumbers."
"And?"
                    "A bowl of fruit. Apples and pears."

Report of Antiphilus of Byzantium

Greek Anthology, IX, 14

Phaedo noticed, sliding along in the shallows,
an octopus that he poked and flipped with an oar
onto the beach grass where, in one of the hollows,
a rabbit had made its burrow close to the shore.

The octopus with a tentacle managed to seize
the rabbit and, in its mortal anguish, squeeze
that creature to death, as Phaedo, astonished, hovered
nearby . . . and thus was surf-and-turf discovered.

Two Epigrams of Abraham Ibn Ezra

The signs at my birth were bad and the constellations
adverse: if I tried to sell candles, as long as I live,
    the sun wouldn't set.

The stars are against me. Nothing I do can succeed:
if I were to deal in shrouds, as long as I live,
    no one would die.

Bram Stoker's Dracula

The blood libel will not stay dead: like the count,
it returns to prey on us, as they imagine
Vlad preys on their daughters. . . .

                              Or let us speak clearly:
we prey on their daughters. From Eastern Europe,

with accents, but looking enough like them to pass?
It's the Jew they fear, that revenant, survivor.
We're what they worry about. "The blood is the life,"
they recognize from our scripture that they have adopted

but cannot or will not understand. The cross
from which the vampire shrinks (in fear? distaste?
or dismay at the unmetaphorical revelation)

is never enough; it's the wooden stake in the end
that they drive through our hearts, they think for England's sake,
to keep it healthy, safe, and *Judenrein.*

The Battle against Humbaba

So far, so good, but I wait for word
that Gilgamesh or Enkidu
will send for me one day to join them

to fight the monster Humbaba, who waits
for us all with his visage like coiling guts.
I am no hero of epic, nor even

a minor player whose name appears
once in the text and again in the index.
But Humbaba looms, and sooner or later,

I shall confront him whose shout is the roar
of the hurricane wave that overwhelms
the fishermen's huts on the beach and the houses

of merchants inland, whose coffers of gold
cannot protect them. I shall go forth
(or else he will come to me) to do battle

to suffer the agonies heroes suffer
and lie as Enkidu lay, so dead
that Gilgamesh saw the maggot fall

out of the nose and knew then to stop
his weeping at last and bury the body.
You don't believe me? Only wait

and you, too, will hear the horrid tread
in the still of the night of Humbaba's approach.
As long as you can, you'll laugh it off,

but that doesn't stop him. Lock the doors
and set the alarm—but it does no good:
Humbaba comes to fight and win.

Vacation Clerihews

Louis Treize
liked to lead the court in Simon Says.
"Simon says, 'Do this!' Simon says, 'Do that!' Simon says,
    'Do this!' Do that!" he'd shout,
and, because he was king, the courtiers did, and of course,
    were all out.

Galileo Galilei
knew that one day
the truth of all his theories would be proved,
and it was, and the church, like the earth it stood on, moved.

Aeneas Sylvanus Piccolomini
served with discretion so many
powerful men by whom he was reckoned
infallible, he became Pius II.

Galleazzo Maria Sforza
was, by all reports, a
dreadfully silly, sadistic, vainglorious man
who, for his sins, or his people's, was Duke of Milan.

Spite

The plot having failed, Jacopo de' Pazzi fled
to Castagno, I think, but they recognized him, seized him,
and dragged him back to Florence. There he was tortured
until, at the end, they hanged him, naked of course,
from a high Signoria window. They cut him down,
and in Santa Croce, at least for a while, he was buried.
But the weather was bad, too wet, and the populace blamed
his malign spirit: they dug him up and dragged him
out of town and dumped the corpse in a handy ditch
by an apple orchard. It lay for a time there, but mobs
have changeable moods, and this one came back, reclaimed him,
and hauled him back through the streets. At the Pazzi Palace,
they propped what was left of the trunk against the *portone*
and, employing the decomposing head as a knocker,
banged as they jeered that the master is home and wishes
to enter. At length, they tired of this and flung
what remained into the Arno. It floated downstream,
where children fished it out to use as a plaything,
stringing it up in a tree, where they beat it with sticks
until they were bored and they dumped it back in the river.
I think of this story sometimes with a certain pleasure,
for as I imagine Jacopo de' Pazzi's face—
in the early stages at least—it looks much like yours.

Moses

If Moses could not enter, which of us can presume?

His offense was striking the rock. But where does it say
that to strike a rock is forbidden? And what harm did he do
to the rock, which, anyway, gave the precious water?
His defect, I fear, was more grave—an excess of goodness
that common sense would suggest is where we should look
in such a man, against whom, it is said, "the angels
banded together."
                              Because he had brought from heaven
the mighty mainstay, the Torah. His act did not
diminish heaven so much as elevate earth—
but still, from then on, the separation was less.

No ravening birds swarmed to tear at his liver
on a mountainside in the frozen north. Such stories,
too vivid, too violent, are not for us. But Jokhebed
cried aloud and looked in the valley of Moab
for the burial place, but it was nowhere to be seen.

She could not weep at his tomb, could not recite
the proper prayers, and her heart was sore, and in heaven
he knew, and cried aloud, "Jokhebed, my mother!"
loud and bitter, as if he were not in heaven,
as if there, too, he had not been permitted entrance.

Cain

I'm not the deplorable fellow you take me for.
Don't be so sure, so quick to judge. Think,
at least for a moment. What did I do? It says,
"Cain rose up against Abel his brother and slew him,"
but where before that can you find that this was forbidden?
I hit him. To use the fancier word, I smote him,
but . . . who knew about death? Of animals, sure,
but were we animals too? It's still a fair question,
and it wasn't at all clear at the time that people
could also die. So "smiting" is what I'll plead to,
and even for that, I can claim I had good reason.

We'd brought our gifts to Yahweh, he and I,
mine the fruit of the soil, because I was a farmer,
and his a lamb—a terrible thing to do.
To take an innocent lamb and cut its throat
for no good reason? Disgusting. You don't do that.
(Or to be precise, you don't do that anymore.)
But Yahweh approved of the gift of this bloody carcass,
and mine, the fruit of my labor, the fruit of the field,
He scorned. He spurned. What kind of god does that?
Unfair, and also wrong. And I was embarrassed
for God's sake as much as anything else,
and stared at the ground—that earth which I had tilled
and on which I'd raised my crop that He'd just rejected.
And Yahweh had the nerve to scold me and yammer
all kinds of nonsense—sin and lust and the need
for self-control. What sin? I'd come with a gift!
What lust? You have to wonder sometimes if Yahweh
is right in the head, which is what I said to Abel—
who could have agreed or at least kept quiet. A brother
owes a brother that much, but he told me how God
had spoken, and preened and put on airs. A brother
can be, as some of you know, a great pain in the ass.
He pissed me off, and I picked up a rock and, yes,
smote the son of a bitch, to let him know
how the poor lamb must have felt and let him consider

how much or little his God's approval meant.
If God made me, this was how He made me,
rational, so that I know what's right and fair,
and, when I'm wronged, hot-headed and even violent.
I am not ashamed. And when Yahweh sent me away
to the land of Nod, to wander east of Eden,
it would be a lie if I said I was sorry to go.

At Snowbird

The scurry of prairie dogs and more earnest marmots'
munching across the Alpine meadow appear
blithe. And the mule deer, ambling into the clearing,
fearless, incurious even (it has seen
hikers before) suggests that peaceable kingdom
we may not believe in but yearn for still: we pause
to take in the mountains' breathtaking otherness,
the evergreen tang in the air, the white-noise rush
of snowmelt rivulets some clever set designer
thought might go just here. (Thus, we distrust
our eyes, our ears, the skin on the back of the neck
where the midmorning sun assures us, as fond fathers
would their fortunate sons, that all is well.)
But mind is working—the prairie dogs and marmots
know, never forget, and forage faster
for the sound of that rushing water, the noise time makes,
the year's turning, the end of the food and warmth:
winter is coming. They are the ones, if they stopped
a moment to look at us, frivolous, blithe, who would gape
at our getups' funny hats and impressive boots.
We do not hibernate; we do not migrate
up the mountain or down as the seasons change—
as if we were still in Eden, or had just stepped out.

Cape Cod Beach

The flashing green light at the Wychmere jetty
seems in this fog to forget from time to time
its business—announcing where we are and the danger
the rocks pose at the harbor's entrance. The years
will bring to us all such moments, but I can remember
only too clearly glaring sun on this sand
where we spread our blankets, or sailing out there on the water,
blue years ago, but black and cold now, where a huge

fog bank looms twenty yards or so offshore
like some nocturnal predator with a taste
for happy times and places. Let it come
to devour at last what remains of this strip of beach,
children at play in that dazzling sun, and loss
for which it is stupid to think these waves still sigh.

II

Readers

1

The words are easy
enough, and even the thoughts
will come if I call

in the proper way,
neither too modest nor too
much overbearing;

the trick is elsewhere,
in conjuring up somehow
that convivial

group with the taste and
requisite cultivation,
but still the gift of

childish playfulness,
whom I try to imagine,
possibilities

who may be figments
but can deign, as angels or
ghosts are said to do

sometimes, to put on
rags of the flesh and appear
before us to grace

what in our despair
we suppose is the real (or,
worse, the only) world.

2

Talent, persistence,
but more than either of these,
luck is what it takes.

And hope? Unless its
fires are banked, it is too much
to bear at these odds.

Still one imagines
schoolchildren with essays to
write, looking up words

and making their notes,
or even, in time to come,
some in search of mere

amusement, their hands,
their eyes, almost at random,
alighting on this,

and finding that, yes,
somehow it speaks in the voice
of an old, close friend.

Sir, madam, I greet
you and presume to send a
bearhug across the

dark gulf of time and
space and the isolation
of each human heart.

3

They are vivid as
one could want, but then will fade,
a special effect

that leaves you alone,
the pen in your hand pointless—
you feel like a fool,

going on this way,
talking to no one or, worse,
to a hole in space,

an emptiness you
can almost feel in the room
you spend your life in.

That garrulity,
useful when you were young, has
grown burdensome now,

as memorized prayers
must be to one who has lost
his last shred of faith.

At moments of stress—
grief or joy—how does he keep
the unbidden words

from burning the tongue
like the stomach's reflux that
can torment his nights?

They may yet return,
but it won't be the same: you
no longer trust them,

and that space in the
room will always remain in
the house of your soul.

Culls

1

What could I have been thinking? (Was it thinking?)

Fantasy, say, or an aspiration: to be
better read. To be better. More thorough, more
generous in my tastes and interests. But this
welter of books I will never look at again
in this life or any other a Shirley MacLaine
might dream up, coming back, time after time . . .

What's strange is the appetite I must once have had:
that voracity's gone now. The gift of age
is taste or, say, an exquisite distaste.

I cannot imagine ever wanting to look at
a poem by—for example—Donald Hall
or Peter Davison, or . . . (fill in the blanks).
By such honest judgments, exercised often,
these piles on the tops of bookcases, on floors,
even under chairs, might be at least reduced.
If I don't do it, my wife someday or my children
will have to paw through this incoherent heap.

Who wants it? Who could ever have wanted this?

*An interrogative pause. And an unsentimental
declarative silence.* With which one cannot argue.

On the shelf in my head are the few books I live with.
Chaucer's clerk of Oxenford had twenty,
which sounds about right. (Chaucer's is one of them, surely.)
The rest are failures, the writers' or mine, good manners
would prefer not to admit. Or else, like clothing,
say I have somehow outgrown them. The closet, too,
indicts with its profusion: what was I thinking?

2

The brain adapts. We can no longer memorize
as we used to do. In surfeit, it sulks, rejects
these projects we propose. But this sorting out
and throwing away, it knows and enjoys, the old
dog's new trick that it does all the time. To remember
every moment? Such unrelentingness
of indiscriminate consciousness prefigures
the torments of hell. (But for what we have let go
we can hope for forgiveness, and perhaps forgive ourselves.)

*Which is getting close to the truth we try to avoid
however we can—that life, after all, is finite
and its range of possibilities ever more narrow.*

The light changes: the air is not yet chilly
but feels different; the green of the trees' leaves
is not what it was last week or yesterday,
and we are betrayed by the look of the land on a hillside.

I noticed that change indoors—it was years ago—
in bookstores, or it was in myself in bookstores,
the old eagerness bruised, the invitations
(theirs and mine) more tentative now, more guarded.

When nomads learned to farm and settled down
by a riverbank, cities were born, and soon thereafter
middens: those ancient places are layers of garbage,
and still when I walk the streets, I can feel them shifting
beneath my feet: under the blocks of solid
pavement that rubble heap, unstable, settles.

3

What will I reread, or even consult?
Let us admit that, for all their heft on the shelves,
books are flighty, become souvenirs of themselves,
appealing no longer to intellect and taste
but playing to sentiment. Why else keep on hand

Look Homeward, Angel, except in the hope that the schoolboy
who turned its pages may show up some afternoon?

And what would we have to say to one another?

Still, for his sake, I have lugged this book along
for years, packed and unpacked it, reshelved it, prepared
for a meeting such as I neither expect nor desire.

What remains when we've finished reading a book?
The impression is vague, like the aftertaste of wine
or the scent a woman was wearing that stays in the room,
which seems to remember and then imagine her presence.
Such residues, I used to assume, compounded,
changing, enriching the reader. And an education
was what persists and accumulates. The figure
is homelier now: imagine a porcelain sink
that over the years hard water has stained; look up;
and see what wisdom the face in the mirror has earned.

Thus Mallarmé's disgust when he said he'd read
all the books—it wasn't a boast, the remark
having begun by asserting that flesh was sad.

*Depression . . . but that's a name for truth the doctors
can't admit (to us or themselves) they agree with.*

We learn its trick too well, how literature
can make the world make sense as we get to the end
and for twenty minutes after we've finished a book
when it all coheres. The harmonies of music,
its reliable resolutions, suggest the same
abstract affirmation. A new day dawns,
but insomniacs see that light as indictment, as judgment
of the body's betrayal and, worse, the spirit's failure.
It only reveals the full extent of disaster,
ruin far worse than anything we had imagined—
a hurricane, a flood, a plague, a pogrom.

4

More calmly, with better balance: I am not immortal;
I am not a repository library; I ought not
presume to impose my tastes on my wife or children
and grandchildren. And the books that I discard
I do not destroy but let free to go on their way
to a dealer's limbo to seek their fortunes—perhaps
to gain admission into their version of heaven,
that shelf of the right reader the author imagined.
For this, they were created. What else matters?

Keepers (or books to detain for a time): the tools
of the trade, the grammars, atlases, dictionaries,
and reference works I consult rather than read.
But the category blurs. To the Bible, Shakespeare,
Homer, Virgil, Ovid . . . one goes to look up
more often than just to sit and, in innocence, read,
innocence being the lack of a purpose, question,
or practical prompting. Such motivations are base,
almost dishonest: we want to appear to know more
than we really do. What our fingertips find we let
people suppose we had on the tip of the tongue.

Then books of friends, and of writers I love: Nabokov,
Proust, Faulkner, Calvino, Nooteboom, Perec,
Raphael, Garrett . . . But fiction has moved upstairs,
mostly displaced by fact's more serious claims,
to which, despite my behavior, I give no credence.
Poetry I keep close, in the room with my desk—
to consult or, say, confer with. For company. Prompting?
That, too. In a kind of conversation
I sometimes believe in, the work of others will speak
to elicit answering speech. Even here, sometimes,
I must cull to make room for what keeps coming in.

In the vigor of youth, reckless, we move or divorce,
and slough off, telling ourselves we will start again,
rebuild, improve, refine, but life isn't like that.

Disaster relents, while I flourish and thrive and the shelves
fill up. I ought to be pleased with such aggregation
like Blenheim's or Chantilly's—but mine is messy,
scattershot, impromptu—in character, too.
The bookshelves' burden remains pretty much what it was.
The occasions over the years have changed and the titles,
but inconstancy is the only constant: I see
in my lack of focus and purpose the same deplorable
flightiness I promised—how many times?—
I'd change and apply myself and pay attention. . . .

Did my father ever believe my protestations?
Did I, even as I spoke, believe myself?

5

Even my own books accuse me, their silent,
baleful reproaches an ever heavier burden:
I should have taken greater pains. More time,
more effort, and, face it, more talent, and I could have made them
better. Mostly I've learned to ignore them: the blurred
monument to my underachievement, the offspring
a dysfunctional parent has let loose on the world.
A few I don't dislike. And for some of the others
the small twinge of displeasure that they occasion
isn't their fault or mine but comes from the fate
we endured together—a signal unsuccess
I tell myself, with some degree of truth,
was the publishers' fault, the reviewers', the bookstore buyers',
the public's, the gods'. Across the street in a warehouse,
I have a locker piled high with the out-of-print
remainders I bought cheap but must pay to keep
(for whom?). A regressive tax levied on failure.

Still, for argument's sake, there must be a few
of that spawn I let loose on the world that found somehow,
against all odds, a home—like those spiders that spin
silk filaments on which they can float on the winds
across the Pacific's vastness. Most of them die,
but a few find their remote atoll that luck

or fate had put there—a reef, a few palm trees
from the coconuts the tides had washed ashore,
the paradise their mad genes had predicted.

That home I like to imagine my books may find
is not in my house but in that of some amateur
not in the business—not a writer, reviewer,
editor, critic, or teacher, who every so often
has to do this, go through this dreary process
and cull. Instead, he keeps in his single bookcase
those few volumes he has made part of his life,
that speak to him somehow and in his head
resonate. And one of them is mine.

Performance: An Eclogue

1

A shepherd boy whose sheep
were chewing the cud or asleep
found a reed that would suit
to fashion himself a flute.
Notching the holes, he made
an instrument with which
he might, in the noonday shade,
divert himself. The rich
and sonorous notes astounded
the lad as they resounded
across the meadow. A bird,
enchanted by what it heard,
joined in to harmonize
with its own descanting cries.
It was an agreeable way
to get through a summer's day.

2

Improvising, he played
on the instrument he'd made
variations on tunes and themes
the breeze in the trees proposed
or the babble of rivers and streams.
Then he put it aside and dozed,
but, as he was falling asleep,
he thought of his flock of sheep,
indifferent and stupid there,
and how pleasant it would be to share
his music with women and men
who could better appreciate
his talented playing and then
might even reciprocate
with applause or some small reward
of whatever they could afford.

3

It was, we may all agree, a
perfectly sound idea.
On his next trip into town,
the shepherd boy sat down
in the marketplace to share
with the farmers and craftsmen there
the pretty tunes he could get
from the flute. Impressed, even awed,
they would stop to listen, applaud,
and ask for more. And yet
the shepherd boy, as he blew
on his flute the tunes he'd rehearsed
with the sheep in the meadow, knew
they weren't quite what they'd been
when he'd played for himself for the first
time. His notes weren't thin,
but less rich, somehow, less lush
than out in the meadow's hush.

4

Practice, practice, practice . . .
He supposed he had to. The fact is
his playing developed in style.
He could make an audience smile,
elicit their clapping and fill ver-
y sizable purses with silver,
but each time, when he was done,
and was taking his curtain calls
in the larger and larger halls
he played in, he thought the fun
was less than the last time. Still,
you can't just lie on a hill
and perform for a flock of sheep,
if you want to earn your keep.
He imagined it though, the air
that smelled of grass, that bird,
the brook that was babbling there,
and the music that he'd first heard.

5

His reputation spread
from village to village. They said
he had to appear at court. . . .
Alone? With a pianoforte,
or harp, or a violoncello?
In white tie and tails? Or, better,
in leather puttees and a sweater
of orange, green, and yellow,
and a woolen hat—so he'd look
like a shepherd—and carry a crook!
The music, however, was worse
each time he played. The halls
made him sound tinny and fake.
There were gold coins now in his purse,
but he had forgotten the calls
of the birds flying over the lake
where the brook flowed. Ladies and lords
wearing velvet and jewels and swords
seemed not to notice or care,
but the boy could tell. In despair
he gave it all up at the last
and went back to his hometown,
where he put his instrument down.
Perhaps, when some time had passed,
he thought, he might try it once more,
in innocent joy, as before.

6

What he discovered, however,
was that innocence, once lost, can never
come back. He could no longer play
in an amateur's carefree way.
There has to be someone to pay
a piper; it can't be just sheep
who are chewing the cud, or asleep,
and wouldn't know brilliance or style
if they stepped in it. Yet with his dumb
flock, he had known, for a while,

joy that's a taste of the wisdom
that sooner or later for all
turns bitter, bitter as gall.
But then he got used to it. He
was better off, we may agree,
than the other young shepherds who'd never
shown talent or been at all clever:
in an afternoon's silence, he would
remember the bird and that song
on which they had both played along—
and imagine that he still could.

Two Prophets

for Bill Kent

A sacred calling, but both of them are mortals,
fallible, even foolish, and sooner or later
they meet, the two prophets—so Strabo says—
and in what may have begun in a friendly way,
swap tales, boasting of feats of prognostication:
Mopsus tells his stories for Calchas to match,
and it turns to a competition, each one daring
the other.
      Calchas points to a nearby fig tree
and asks how many he thinks there are.
                              In an instant,
"Ten thousand less one," Mopsus answers,
"Just enough to fill the hold of the ship
arriving at this moment, I do believe,"
and he points a hand vaguely toward the harbor.

A defiantly odd number. They hire a crew
to pick the tree clean, and sure enough,
9,999
figs, and they fit in the hold of the ship. Just.

Now it's Calchas, turn, and Mopsus asks,
"That sow about to farrow . . . Would you perhaps
hazard a guess? The number of piglets? Their gender?"

Calchas, who hasn't the vaguest idea, says so,
annoyed, because this shouldn't be a game.
But Mopsus, who isn't playing, announces, "Ten.
Tomorrow. One, a male, will be all black.
The other nine will be females, streaked with white."

And so it happens. And Calchas is undone.
Destroyed, he dies, we read, "in an excess of grief."

    ∽

As if that business at Aulis were nothing. As if
the puzzling out of the plague at Troy had been nothing.
He is not the *Iliad*'s author or *Oresteia*'s,
but he foretold all their bloody and grand events,
which ought to have weighed in the scale
                              against . . . what?
Figs and pigs!
                    And the deadly worm of envy
that blinds and eats into the soul, that makes
even the profoundest wisdom partial.
What it can make, in the end, is a heavy heart.

                    ∽

The future, we have learned in a hard school,
is misty. The past, where we look for what we love
or are proud of to find that it jostles with shame, is also
misty.
          And who could bear it, otherwise—
clear, plain as day? We walk a knife-edge,
chasms on either side of us, and we learn
never to look down, or almost never.

                    ∽

In the *Argonautica,* there is a similar duel:
Mopsus predicts, as it turns out quite correctly,
much of the bloody business they face and the bloody
consequences: Medea, the butchered babies.
But Idmon gets up and, although he leaves out a lot,
foretells success. The tears running down his cheeks
the crew supposes are those of joy, but we know
better and comprehend their happy error.
We see what he can see: his death. Does Mopsus
resent Idmon's intrusion? Does he see, too?
Not told, we are not prevented from supposing
whatever we prefer or may find congenial.
But we are invited to make it a better story.

                    ∽

The lines in his palm the baby is born with map
the road his feet will travel, but do not peek:

even if you could tell the story, let him
find his own voice. The plot may be fixed,
but he may contrive stylistic variations
no one could have expected, by which he will change
everything, or better, redeem everything,
or at least put it somehow into quotation marks.

Stare into his eyes and let what wisdom
your years have accumulated meet his hopes.
Can you say, positively, which of you is wrong?

&

This habit of leaning into the future is cruel.
Distinction is what we inherit or earn: our status
is always a gift of the status quo, our past
being what we are now. What we may become
is for preachers and politicians, the demagogues,
who threaten or promise. It does not own us yet.

Mopsus' showy tricks are irrelevant, vulgar,
a lounge act. A singer would do as well,
or even a poet, Calchas. But you were undone
nonetheless. It wasn't Mopsus but you,
your own doubts, that required you, every day,
to prove again that you had the god's favor.

As if the gods were constant.
                              As if Apollo
had not, for a time, done duty as Admetos' shepherd.

Apollo knew who he was, but your faith, Calchas,
failed.
        As Mopsus guessed—or foretold—it might.

&

Beyond the lounge, you can hear the casino noises,
the pulling of cranks, the clatter of coins, the bells
when a jackpot hits. The "gaming industry"
isn't a game either. And the money is only
tokens.

What they yearn for, every one,
is the gods' favor. The smiling of fates that have heard
their prayers and been moved to answer. Lacking that,
what of worth can remain, or what other ruin
can matter?
            There is no time, no day or night,
and the garish lights may stand for the stars or flash
like beacons beckoning, warning.
                              Those who have faith
do not require assurance. But we who doubt,
and therefore want the gods, know sacrifice
is necessary—what we ourselves would demand
in the way of worship, penance, and punishment.
Cherries, bars, and lemons. Figs and pigs.
For Mopsus, the big winner, the bells go off
and the management sends him back home in a limo.
For Calchas, the last indignity—the bus
with the other losers. That's what did him in.

Against Landscape

Nature has no outline, but Imagination has.
—William Blake, *Notebooks*

1

Trees, bushes, grass, sky . . . they are stupid,
but to compensate we invest them with what we think,
endow them with meaning, make much of their little,

and turn their inert donné into something that shimmers
with the life we suppose must be there, as pagans did
with peekaboo naiads and dryads at every turn.

Or we make the world's body a woman's and love it,
exchanging at once a remarkable paysage
for passion's banal blur, a young man's longing

for what's unseen: we settle for metaphor.
Impatient, or ill at ease in such moments of stillness,
we intrude and whistle up our own birdsong.

2

We lean toward this, like a tree steady onshore winds
have bent to the picturesque, or is it away
from the brute truth, that we are headed there,

will become, when enough of those glossy calendar pages
have blown away, a part of their advertised landscape
in some hole in the ground or wraith of smoke in the air

and an urn full of ashes: an end, at last, of thinking,
which may not yet be the truth but will serve it better
than connoisseurs can imagine? What in nature

presumes to appreciate sea scenes or sunsets
and, whipping out notebook and pencil or camera or paint,
thinks to approve or impose or even preserve?

3

Whatever shadows conceal, we supply; whatever
reflection provides, although we may find it amusing,
we try to discount as ephemeral, artifact.

A field of vision remains, nonetheless, a field
that tricks of the urbane eye cannot cultivate
enough. What we drag indoors to hang on the wall

is something else. The darkness and bright glint,
the scale, the composition, the organization
of balancing geometrical shapes is not at all

it but only diversion, decoration,
horseshit without the smell and with nothing for birds,
desperate with hunger, to peck through for something good.

4

But home ground, where the winding paths your feet
have worn through the scrub are tracked, too, into your brain?
What you feel for this place, though you call it, imprecisely,

love, is a sense that the dangers are less, or known,
and that having found food and shelter here, having survived,
you may hope to continue to do so. The roadside shrines

or dried-out wreaths survivors have left to mark
their catastrophes, you shrug off or ignore:
what has someone else's fate to do with you?

And you're right, for a change. From that taste of indifference, learn
how not to feel. In the unblinking eye of the sun
remote overhead, there is nothing at last but blindness.

5

It's leisure that does us in, improving, corrupting
our vision: we cultivate nothing but taste. What hunters
and, later, farmers learned, we are proud to forget,

delighting in mountains too steep for vines, or stark
deserts, or shorelines too craggy for any boat
to negotiate. We have never known more of hunger

than peckishness. And at pilgrims' holy places
we visit merely as tourists, though not ill-informed.
I have put my hand on the Wailing Wall and trudged

up Delphi's hill, but their ancient stones were mute
and not especially pretty. The stone of my heart
didn't sunder, melt, or even perceptibly soften.

6

But in China, the five sacred mountains the son
of heaven had to visit to demonstrate
that he had received the mandate? They imagined

pillars connecting this terrestrial realm
with the higher and lower, and K'un Lun, being the most
remote, was the most holy: immortals dwelt there

(guarded by tigers and, higher up, dragons), transcendent,
transparent, dissolved somehow in the breath of *ch'i,*
and able to ride on storks or tread thin air. . . .

In other words, not real, except in that yearning
for elsewhere, other, not these untranscendent
streets and fields we sweat on until we drop.

7

Not that otherness doesn't impend: we live
in the shadows of beetling heights—Sinai, Zion,
Pisgah, Carmel, Ararat, Golgotha—

but even such mountains as those in time wear down
to the unremarkable hills civil engineers
who understand rock put highways around and through.

The clouds that obscure their peaks blow away, come back,
blow away again, betrayed by whims of weather.
We look up, willing to take any passing suggestion

as truth, but the sky keeps changing. Those brave or foolish
souls who have made the climb descend to report
how cold, how high it was. As we might have guessed.

A Zemerl for Rabbi Nachman

1 Rabbi Nachman Goes into the Woods

He would go, in his brokenheartedness, into the woods
every day, as if he had an appointment
to talk for an hour to God, speaking in Yiddish,
or maybe not speaking, but only repeating one word,

or less than a word, a syllable, a single
vowel, a howl, a pure vocalization,
from which he expected little result. "Zimzum,"
God's apartness, or say, His withdrawal, requires

drastic, desperate measures, and Rabbi Nachman's
keening out in the woods he believed would work
like water that can wear away a stone.

The stone, he said, is the heart—not God's, but his own,
which little by little he might contrive to soften,
to open again, soothed, or even healed.

2 The Rabbi in Town

But in town, what? In Bratslav or Zlatipolia,
surrounded by crowds? What can one do?
                                        Try
to take some comfort: a single person's prayers
God may reject; but in shul, in a minyan, bound up
with the prayers and the hearts of the others, surely the Lord
will hear your supplication.
                              And when that idea
fails to comfort?
                   Then, as the Rebbe said,
"One can dance such a small and delicate dance
that no one can see. And also one can scream
in a still, small voice, making a great scream
that no one else can hear, without a sound,
a scream in the silence, a scream your mind imagines
that penetrates your being. And all being."

3 Equity

Knowing how bad he feels, how much he grieves,
how sharply aware he is of the separation
between himself and God (all knowledge starts
from this), he extorts from this terrible absence
a consolation, extrapolating, to think
how it has to be, at the other end, much worse
for God, who must also grieve cut off from him.

4 Mirrors

The face of the moon reflects the sun's bright light;
so a disciple's face must receive and mirror
the enlightenment of his master, for it is written
in Scripture how the Lord spoke "face to face."*

And the master beholds himself in his pupil's face:
imagine two mirrors in opposition
with their infinite repetitions of one another. . . .
But this, Rabbi Nachman said, only partly in jest,
would be displeasing to heaven. "If God were content
to worship Himself, what need would He have of us?"

5 The Telling of Stories

Science? It comes from the forehead of the snake.
And Reason? The Rebbe called it an imperfection:
for a man to be whole, he must learn to let go, be simple,
and in his descent ascend to faith and joy.

These are subversive ideas that evil men
seize upon and misuse. Therefore, he contrived
a way to reveal his teachings while keeping them hidden—
in stories. Here he could fashion a garbing of wisdom
to trick the unwary. And good for good men, too.
To waken the sleeping spirit, one must go slowly.
Think how it is when a blind man is healed: they give him
a blindfold; they have to protect him from too much light

*Deuteronomy 5:4

that could ruin his sight.
                              In this he had changed his mind.
A younger man, he had fought against fantasy's dangers,
its snares and delusions distractions from truth and faith,
but fantasy, too, is a power that comes from God.

The struggle is not against the imagination
but within its extravagant realm, in its heights and depths.

6 *The Tale of the Man Deep in Debt*

The money itself is the least of it. (Still, the amount
you owe is more than you have or can ever hope for.)
It's the shame that oppresses, the fact that you're forced to admit
you're a failure, a fool, have been weighed and found wanting. Poor,
you are, as the world reckons, of no account,
a zero, worthless, of negative worth, an abject
object of scorn and derision your neighbors point to,
warning their sons not to grow up to be like you.

Of that shame, he was connoisseur; of that utter dejection
he was the master. In stories a man tells
are the snares his heart has thrashed in, and Rabbi Nachman's
woe is here in its richness.
                              "And then what happens?"
is the question we learned as little children to ask.

The rabbi tells us how the poor man at last
is brought in his shame and terror into the office
where the rich moneylender to whom he owes more than his all
sits and hears him out as he stammers excuses,
lame, unpersuasive, even to his own ears
as he mouths the bitter words.
                              But the terrible judgment
does not come. Instead, the man waves his hand,
explains he has millions, and says that he doesn't care.
The debt is trivial, nothing to worry about,
and the poor debtor feels both relieved and insulted.
The rich man, seeing this, as an act of kindness
suggests, "There is a way you might work off
the debt, for others owe me sizable sums.

If you will go to my other debtors, remind them
their payments are overdue, and try to collect,
you will bring me hundreds of times what you owe. Agreed?"

Of course.
        It's the *rebbe*, the man who owes—not money
but a moral debt. And the moneylender is God,
blessed be He. And this is how, with his defects,
Nachman presumes to preach and teach, to remind
us others how much we owe, and to whom, and how
we ought perhaps to consider some partial payment.

Angel of Death

An abrupt silence no deaf man could dream of,
a sudden darkness no blind man could fear,
and a breathlessness of a focused attention that fades . . .

I always supposed it would be like that. Now, weathered,
but hardly wiser, I cannot improve or refine
that child's idea of dying. It oughtn't be
subtle: even the stupid contrive in the end
to accomplish that mortal feat—falling off a log.
(But never hitting the ground, the fall going on
forever?) Something like this is what she sidles
up to, drifting off again to a nap,
as if for practice.
                    The tongue seeks out a tooth's
rough place, and the mind reverts to an irregularity,
as if by such usage to lick it smooth. It never
works; the snag persists; there's a run
in the future's nylons.

What's left in hand is not even good for rags.

   ∾

The name in Hebrew? My daughter-in-law is asking
so she can pray for her.
                    She never had one,
or never knew or doesn't remember.
(She doesn't remember a lot.)

For *Barbara*? *Bracha*, maybe? "Blessing?"
Or we could go for the meaning:
"stranger"—*Gershona*, the feminine version
of the name of Moses' son, who was
"born in a foreign land."
(And the patronym? Uncle Dick's
Hebrew name? We can get that
perhaps from her brother's headstone.)

Which of us here in this light is not a stranger?

∽

Socrates said death is no misfortune.
Most men would like to believe this but cannot.
We bear the cost of language, which can suppose
whatever we like, or hate, or can imagine.
(And imagination is often of what is not.)

∽

The terror is not in the dying but in the mind,
the brain—and hers is riddled, rattled, raddled,
radiated. She frets but cannot remember:
did she take her medicine? merely think to do so?
It makes no difference. She is beyond cure,
but not beyond care. . . .
                              As if her survival
depended somehow on her being a good girl,
she thinks if she does what she's told, nothing bad
will happen to her.
                              This is what she assumes
and has always lived by.
                              It is not so.

∽

Another stranger waits, meanwhile,
at the furry tent-flap. One day this week, or next,
he or she will appear and, in what looks like
rage, with small clenched fists will cry and blink.
And who can say it is not with cause?
Was it Sophocles or Hesiod who said,
"What is best is never to have been born"?
Both, I'm afraid.

∽

Across a leaden sky, three arrowheads:
Canada geese, on their way south. How do they
know where they're going? How do they choose
their squadron leaders? I am on cruise control,
but so are they, tending better than I can
to destinies for which they cannot imagine
alternatives, and in their sure
purposiveness, would not, even if geese could.

I envy that, but my car, going up a hill,
shifts to maintain its speed. My body, too,
responds to its own system controls.
Mostly, I don't even know when it changes gear.

Those arrowheads have written on the sky . . .
A warning? A word of comfort?
                                        A statement of fact.
The baby, Barbara, and I are all in formation,
which is all the information anyone needs.

Do I believe that?

Does it make any difference what I believe?

                ∞

The baby, due at the solstice, had to have been
conceived at the equinox—around my birthday,
as I would have been begun at the summer solstice.
Does that coincidence make us closer kin,
give us some special connection?
Not at all—unless one of us thinks so.

                ∞

After a stillbirth, or after an infant death,
the next child, some primitive tribes believe,
is stronger, bearing both lives, its spirit cagey,
having been here a while already to scout the terrain.

It's true, of course, for these "replacement children"—
which is what they're called—get special love and attention,
a doting another child could never imagine.
They are, for the rest of their lives, princes, princesses.

And here, when a birth and a death coincide?
                                        It's hard
not to suppose some balancing out of accounts
as we see how, at almost the same moment,
the Lord giveth and taketh away.

Such consolations are stupid.
                                        But better than none.

Barbara called last night: her right side
is weak, she has trouble walking, trouble
getting up out of bed.

This morning, when we telephone to ask
how she's doing, she can't remember
the call she made last night.
Trouble.

And twenty minutes later . . .
but this time it isn't Barbara.
Now it's Josh. From the hospital:
Nadine's water has broken.

For unto us a child is born.
Unto us a son is given.
And his name shall be called
Samuel.
My father's name. And Nadine's father's father's.
"Asked of God," as every child should be.

I hold him in my arms, the precious, breathing
weight, and admire the tiny hands
that will bear the weight one day of my coffin's corner.
Two sons and two grandsons . . . Thanks be to God.
That a Sam once more will carry me is a comfort.

But that's far off.
Barbara, who takes much shorter views,
receives my news with moderated pleasure.
"I'll try to remember," she says.

She has other things on her mind
(what's left of her mind)—
these unsayable things that I have been thinking.
She has been thinking, too. We are children again,
playing at musical chairs. The music is stopping.

Someone is taking her place.

This is also, I realize, my father's yahrzeit. . . .
The first few years, I used to light a candle,
but I gave it up. Still, I would always feel
some twinge of guilt—enough to be annoying.
One learns to live with that; now I won't have to.
This is his candle, my grandson, his namesake,
shining with a new lifetime of light.

∽

Time passes, a month, another. Barbara
has stabilized. "At a somewhat lower level
than we might have hoped," is how a doctor puts it.
With the help of a walker, she can get around her apartment.
Once, when the weather was good, she went to a movie.
Two men carried her down the stairs in a chair
and then, in the ambulette, to the movie theater,
and home again. She remembers the film and liked it,
but cannot think of the name. She complains of boredom.

∽

We, too, are bored, but cannot say so. Grief
has its own pace and rhythm. We've moved along,
but she is stuck where she was, hangs on like a leaf
on a tree in winter, waiting, daring the wind.

Sam, meanwhile, has outgrown his first baby clothes.
Yesterday, he turned himself over, that first
assertion of will and control in a difficult world.

∽

A plateau, the doctors call it, and yet it tilts
ever so slightly downward. As whose does not?
My birthday has come and gone and the vernal
equinox. It isn't Sam but myself
I think of. The burgeoning spring is his. For us
it is that time of the fall, exhilarating
but chastening, when we wait for the killing frost.

∽

I am looking for this evening's concert tickets.
I am drinking coffee. I have been reading proof. I am
interrupted. The phone rings.
                              It is midmorning.
Early calls are frightening. Late ones, too.
Wrong numbers, as often as not. But the Angel of Death
telephones these days, and good news keeps
for a civilized hour.

Without apprehension, I answer.
The word from the hospice director: "deterioration."
Her right side's all but gone. She has "some pain"
in her back (which could be spinal mets). She is frightened.
The question is whether to hospitalize her now.
No, I say, because that would frighten her more.
The apartment is familiar. Keep her there.

Neither of us has spoken the other dire
word that hangs in the air,
but she will die at home.

        ❧

"Deterioration" means:

        Catheterized. She has trouble otherwise
passing urine. It could be the pain meds.
It could be tumor, obstructing, somehow,
the urethra. Or neurologic, a difficulty
in getting commands through
from scrambled brain to wasted body.

        Bed-ridden. She fell again, was that sack
of meal I remember from a visit some months ago
when her legs gave way. Two passing Samaritans
helped me get her on her feet again.
That was before the walker, before the chairs,
motorized to help her stand up. Now,
she is in a hospital bed from which she will never
arise. In weeks or days, men in black suits
will carry that sack away.

∽

She is "agitated," afraid. And Ativan
doesn't work, or does "paradoxically,"
making her feel even worse. So what do they have
to fall back on? The next word in the curt
sentence is the grim relief, morphine. . .

∽

Monday night, on the phone, she cries, afraid.
Tuesday, I don't call. None of us does.

Wednesday, they call us to announce it's over.

Driving home from the end-of-the-term party,
I had seen, on the side of the road, a doe's carcass,
not fifty feet from one of those caution signs
with a bounding buck on a yellow diamond.
                                        Barbara's
plight, I thought. The signs do no damn good.
They tell us what we already know.

At home, a part of me knew, before I heard
the words, that Barbara was dead.
In her sleep, she just stopped breathing.

∽

This morning, in the yard, the first iris
has opened, burst its green pod, showing forth
its royal purple flag, her favorite color.
Another sign? It could be, if I believed it,
but does that do me any good? Or her?

And then I catch myself. What I can believe
is grammatical rules. That present tense has departed
along with her and is wrong. All her verbs now
are in the imperfect, perfect, and pluperfect,
what she was, has been, what she had been.

In Poland

The pine trees, stately, correct beneath gray sky,
and the dull green grass, still splotched with tatters of snow
that has lasted well into March, seem not to acknowledge
where we are, let alone apologize,
and they cannot even begin to explain Treblinka.
Nor do they console. At most, they suggest patience
in the way they stand there, enduring a cutting wind
and deaf to its moans as, stoic, they wait for the weather
to change and bring that warmth they have bet their lives on
and that may, in heaven's sweet time, return, even here.